Creative Art & Activities Clay, Play Dough, and Modeling Materials

Mary Mayesky

THOMSON

DELMAR LEARNING

Australia   Canada   Mexico   Singapore   Spain   United Kingdom   United States

THOMSON

DELMAR LEARNING

Creative Art and Activities: Clay, Play Dough, and Modeling Materials
Mary Mayesky

Vice President, Career Ed SBU:
Dawn Gerrain

Director of Editorial:
Sherry Gomoll

Acquisitions Editor:
Erin O'Connor

Developmental Editor:
Alexis Ferraro

Editorial Assistant:
Ivy Ip

Director of Production:
Wendy A. Troeger

Production Coordinator:
Nina Tucciarelli

Composition:
Stratford Publishing Services

Director of Marketing:
Donna J. Lewis

Cover Design:
Tom Cicero

Library of Congress Cataloging-in-Publication
Data

Mayesky, Mary

1-4018-3476-0

NOTICE TO THE READER

To Jane, thank you for listening, caring, and being there for me.

With love, Mary

Contents

Introduction

Welcome to the world of clay and play dough! At all ages, work with clay and play dough gives children many chances for creative experiences. Most children like the damp feel of clay. They like to pound it, roll it, poke holes in it, and pull it apart.

The activities in this book are designed for children aged 2 through 8. An icon representing a suggested age for the activity is listed at the top of each activity. However, use your knowledge of the child's abilities to guide you in choosing and using the activities in this book. Wherever appropriate, information is provided on how to adapt the activity for children over age 8.

Through working with clay and play dough, children can express their creativity and discover and build their own unique styles of expression. Each child's work with clay differs from another child's, just as children's appearances and personalities differ.

Children who see clay as "messy" or "slimy" may not want to work with it. Never force the issue. Be patient and give these children lots of time and plenty of opportunities to see the fun others have with clay. Some adults find that involving timid children first in a "cleaner" aspect of clay work, such as mixing play dough, helps involve those children gradually. Hesitant children might feel more comfortable sitting near you as you pat the dough and describe how it feels. Acknowledge these simple participations. Eventually, when hesitant children feel more comfortable, they may try patting gently with you or a friend.

GETTING STARTED

Process vs. Product

The focus of this book and all early childhood art activities is on process, not product. This means that the process of creating, not the product, is the main reason for the activity. The joys of creating, exploring materials, and discovering how things look and work are all part of the creative process. How the product looks, what it is "supposed to be," is unimportant to the child, and it should be unimportant to the adult.

Young children delight in the experience, the exploration, and the experimentation of art activities. The adult's role is to provide interesting materials and an environment that encourages children's creativity. Stand back when you are tempted to "help" children working with clay. Instead, encourage all children to discover their own unique abilities.

Clay and play dough are especially good for creative expression because they are plastic materials, which means they are flexible. They can be rolled into one form, smashed, and then become another. This soft, plastic quality of clay and dough appeals to children of all ages.

Young children generally use dough and clay again and again rather than make and take objects home.

For special occasions, however, it is nice to allow pieces to harden and to then paint or color them. Two recipes in this book serve this purpose particularly well: Ornamental Clay and Baker's Dough.

Considering the Child

Young children find it hard to wait patiently to use materials in an activity. Often, the excitement of creativity and patience do not mix. In addition, it is sometimes difficult for young children to share. With young children, plan to have enough materials for each child. For example, having enough play dough for each child makes activities more fun and relaxed for young children.

Gathering Materials

Each activity in this book includes a list of required materials. It is important to gather all materials before starting an activity with children. Children's creative experiences are easily discouraged when they must sit and wait while the adult looks for play dough materials. Be sure to gather materials in a place the children can easily access. See **Figure 1** for more ideas on storing art materials.

Using Food Products

Many of the play dough recipes in this book involve the use of food. There are long-standing arguments for and against food use in art activities. For example, many teachers have long used potato printing as a traditional printing activity for young children. These teachers feel potatoes are an economical way to prepare printing objects for children. Using potatoes beyond their shelf life is an alternative to throwing them away. On the other hand, many teachers feel that food is for eating and should be used for nothing else.

This book has many activities that do not use food so that there will be options for teachers who oppose the use of food in art activities. Also, where possible, alternatives to food items are suggested. Whatever your opinion, creative activities in clay and dough are provided for your and the children's exploration and enjoyment.

You will also find recipes in this book for edible and nonedible play doughs. Edible play dough activities are marked with a smiley face with a tongue. When experiencing both kinds of activities, young children may be unclear as to what they can and cannot eat. When conducting these activities, take the time to talk with the children about which things they may taste and which they may not. For example, when making anything mixed with glue, remind the children that glue is not to be tasted.

To help remind young children about what they can and cannot eat, you may find it helpful to display an icon like the one used in this book. To show a "no-taste" activity, use the same smiley face icon under a large, black X. Displaying and reminding the children about the meanings of these symbols can help children avoid confusion about what they can and cannot taste.

Employing Safe Materials

For all activities in this book and for any art activities for young children, be sure to use safe art supplies. Read labels on all art materials. Check materials for age appropriateness. The Art and Creative Materials Institute (ACMI) labels art materials AP (approved product) and CL (certified label). Products with these labels are certified safe for use by young children.

FIGURE 1 · TIPS FOR STORING ART MATERIALS

The ways materials, supplies, and space are arranged can make or break children's and teachers' art experiences. Following are suggestions for arranging supplies for art experiences:

1. *Scissor holders*. Holders can be made from gallon milk or bleach containers. Simply punch holes in the containers and place scissors in the holes with the scissor points to the inside. Egg cartons turned upside down with slits in each mound also make excellent holders.

2. *Paint containers*. Containers can range from muffin tins and plastic egg cartons to plastic soft-drink cartons with baby food jars in them. These work especially well outdoors as well as indoors, because they are large and not easily tipped. Place one brush in each container. This prevents colors from mixing and makes cleanup easier.

3. *Crayon containers*. Juice and vegetable cans painted or covered with contact paper work very well.

4. Crayon pieces may be melted in muffin trays in a warm oven. These pieces, when cooled, are nice for rubbings or drawings. Crayola® makes a unit that is designed specifically for melting crayons safely.

5. Printing with tempera is easier if the tray is lined with a sponge or a paper towel.

6. A card file for art activities helps organize the program.

7. *Clay containers*. Airtight coffee cans and plastic food containers are excellent ways to keep clay moist and always ready for use.

8. *Paper scrap boxes*. By keeping two or more boxes of scrap paper of different sizes, children will be able to choose the size paper they want more easily.

9. Cover a wall area with pegboard and suspend heavy shopping bags or transparent plastic bags from hooks inserted in the pegboard to hold miscellaneous art supplies. Hang smocks in the same way on the pegboard (at child level, of course).

10. Use the back of a piano or bookcase to hang a shoe bag. Its pockets can hold many small items.

11. Use divided frozen food trays or a revolving lazy Susan to hold miscellaneous small items.

(From Mayesky, Mary. *Creative Activites for Young Children*, 7th ed., Clifton Park, NY: Delmar Learning.)

The ACMI provides an extensive list of materials and manufacturers of safe materials for all young children. This information is available on the ACMI Web site at http://www.acminet.org or by writing to 715 Boylston Street, Boston, MA 02116.

Some basic safety hints for art activities are:

- Always use products that are appropriate for the child. Use nontoxic materials for children in grades 6 and lower.

- Never use products for skin painting or food preparation unless the products are intended for those uses.

- Do not transfer art materials to other containers. You will lose the valuable safety information on the product packages.

- Do not eat or drink while using art and craft materials. Wash after use. Clean yourself and your supplies.

- Be sure that your work area is well ventilated.

Potentially unsafe art supplies for clay and play dough activities include:

- *Powdered clay.* Powdered clay is easily inhaled and contains silica, which harms the lungs. Instead, use wet clay, which cannot be inhaled.

- *Instant papier-mâché.* Instant papier-mâché may contain lead or asbestos. Use only black-and-white newspaper and library paste or liquid starch.

- *Epoxy, instant glues, or other solvent-based glues.* Use only water-based, white glue.

- *Paints that require solvents like turpentine to clean.* Use only water-based paints.

- *Cold water or commercial dyes that contain chemical additives.* Use only natural vegetable dyes made from beets, onion skins, and so on.

- *Permanent markers.* Permanent makers may contain toxic solvents. Use only water-based markers.

Be aware of all children's allergies. Children with allergies to wheat, for example, may be irritated by the wheat paste used in papier-mâché. Children allergic to peanuts must taste nothing with peanut butter. In fact, some centers make it a rule to avoid all peanut butter use in food or art activities. Other art materials that may cause allergic reactions include chalk or other dusty substances, water-based clay, and any material that contains petroleum products.

In addition to children's allergies, be aware of children's habits. Some young children put everything in their mouths. (This can be the case at any age.) Others may be shy and slow to accept new materials. Use your knowledge of children's tendencies to help you plan art activities that are safe for all children.

Creating a Child-Friendly Environment

It is difficult to be creative when you have to worry about keeping yourself and your work area clean. Remember to cover the children. Some good cover-ups are men's shirts (with the sleeves cut off), aprons, pillowcases with holes cut for the head and arms, and smocks. Some fun alternatives are sets of old clothes or shoes that can be worn as "art clothes." These old clothes could become "art journals" as they became covered with the traces of various art projects.

Creating a Child's Art Environment

Encourage young artists by displaying appropriate art prints and other works of art. Do not make the mistake of thinking young children do not enjoy "grownup" art. Children are never too young to enjoy the colors, lines, patterns, and designs of artists' work. Art posters from a local museum, for example, can brighten an art area. Such posters also get children looking at and talking about art, which encourages the children's creative work.

Display pieces of pottery, shells and rocks, and other beautiful objects from nature to encourage children's appreciation of the lines, symmetries, and colors of nature. These design concepts will be part of the children's clay and play dough experiences. Even the youngest child can enjoy the look and feel of smooth, colored rocks or the colors of fall leaves. All these are natural parts of a child's world that can be talked about with young children as they create art. Enjoying the beautiful objects you display in the room can only encourage the creativity of young children.

Understanding Clay and Play Dough Basics

Working with clay and play dough requires some planning. Without planning and basic information, you may have to constantly remind the children about the proper uses of clay.

Following are some tips for clay and play dough setup:

- Place surfaces for working with clay away from things like wheel and climbing toys. Cover the surfaces with linoleum or formica to make cleaning easier. When tables have formica tops, they usually require no additional covering.

- Young children enjoy working with clay on vinyl placemats, Masonite® boards, burlap squares, or brown-paper grocery bags. Newspaper does not work well, because when it gets wet, bits of paper may mix with the clay.

- For clay that is meant to be hardened and possibly painted later, set up a good drying place. Because clay objects may take a few days to dry, set up this place away from frequently used areas.

- Give each child a lump of clay or play dough at least the size of a large apple or a small grapefruit.

- Do not allow children to throw clay on the floor or to interfere with other children's work.

- As an adult, you may sit at the table and play with clay, too, but avoid making objects for the child to copy. This discourages the child's creative use of clay.

- When the children are done with activities, they must store clay and dough until the materials' next use. Form clay into balls, each about the size of an apple. A hole filled with water in each ball helps keep the clay just right for use the next time. Keep clay in a container with a wet cloth or a sponge over the clay. Cover the container with a tight-fitting lid. (Margarine tubs with plastic lids work well.)

- Clay will grow mold when it is too wet and too hard to handle when it becomes very dry. When clay dries, restore it to proper consistency by placing it in a cloth bag and pounding it with a hammer until it breaks into small pieces. After soaking the pieces in water, knead them to the proper consistency again.

- Clay that has grown mold is salvageable. Simply scrape off the moldy area and drain off any water in the bottom of the container.

- Store play dough in a tightly covered container. No water is needed to keep the dough at proper consistency.

Using Potter's Clay

Potter's clay, which you may purchase at any art supply store in moist form, is much easier to work with than dry powder. Potter's clay is available in two colors: gray and terra-cotta. (Terra-cotta looks pretty but stains clothing and is harder to clean). When oilcloth table covers are used with potter's clay, the covers can simply be hung up to dry, shaken well, and put away until next use.

Making Play Dough

Let the children participate in dough making whenever possible. Through making dough, children learn about measuring and blending and cause and effect, and they have the chance to work together.

Doughs that require no cooking are best mixed two batches at a time in separate deep dishpans. Deep pans keep the flour of the dough within bounds. Making two batches at a time relieves congestion and gives the children a better chance to participate.

Tempera powder is the most effective dough coloring agent, because it makes intense shades. For the best results, add it to the flour before pouring in into the liquid.

Dough can be refrigerated and reused several times. Remove the dough at the beginning of the day to allow it to reach room temperature before use. Otherwise, it can be discouragingly stiff and unappealing. It is usually necessary to add flour or cornstarch on the second day to reduce stickiness.

Cleaning Up

For clay cleanup, sponge off tables, mats, and boards. Burlap squares can be stacked and shaken when dry, and grocery bags can be thrown away. Clay-caked hands and tools should never be washed in the sink, because clay can clog the drain. Instead, have the children wipe off their tools and hands with paper towels, then wash them in a basin filled with soapy water. When the clay particles settle, you can let the soapy water down the drain and throw the pieces of clay in the trashcan. Children may then rinse their hands in the sink. The tools may be left to dry on paper towels.

Cooked-cornstarch recipes are particularly difficult to clean up after because they leave a hard, dry film on the pan during cooking. However, an hour or two of soaking in cold water converts this film to a jellylike material that is easily scrubbed off with a plastic pot-scrubbing pad. You might even have one or two of the children work on scrubbing the pot clean!

Exploring Other Ideas

Working with clay and play dough is considered a modeling or sculpture activity. Sculpture is a three-dimensional art form, which means it is "in the round," or seen on all sides. You will find sculpture activities in this book that include such materials as natural objects, spools, and foil. These activities are included to expand on the traditional sculpture activities with clay and play dough.

Now, prepared with all the preceding information, you can start sharing and enjoying the activities in this book with the children. Enjoy!

Apple Sculptures

MATERIALS

☐ apples
☐ toothpicks
☐ marshmallows
☐ raisins

HELPFUL HINT

- Be prepared for young artists who would rather eat the "details" rather than use them to decorate. This is part of the fun!

DEVELOPMENTAL GOALS

Develop creativity, small motor development, and hand-eye coordination and explore a new kind of sculpture material.

PREPARATION

Instruct children to wash their hands. Break the toothpicks into small pieces.

PROCESS

1. Give each child an apple.
2. Use tiny bits of toothpicks for attaching to the apple.
3. Attach raisins and marshmallows for details.
4. Use whole toothpicks for arms and legs.
5. Display the apple creations until snack time.
6. Enjoy the apple creation for snack!

VARIATIONS

- Make an orange or a pear creation.
- Make favorite animals or storybook characters from apples or other fruit.
- Older children can create a group of apple characters for a short play or story presentation.
- Children under 3 years can add details to the apples with cream cheese or peanut butter instead of toothpicks.

NOTES FOR NEXT TIME: _____

_____

_____

_____

Baker's Dough

MATERIALS

- ☐ 4 cups flour
- ☐ 1 to 1-1/2 cups water
- ☐ 1 cup salt
- ☐ bowl, spoon for stirring
- ☐ measuring cups

💡 HELPFUL HINTS

- This activity is suitable for dried objects.
- Be careful that children do not touch the warm oven. Have constant adult supervision during the baking process.
- The dough will brown slightly, but baking at lower temperatures is not as successful.
- The children can safely taste this dough, but it is not very yummy!

DEVELOPMENTAL GOALS

Develop creativity, small motor development, and hand-eye coordination; explore a new kind of dough; and reinforce physical changes in materials during mixing.

PREPARATION

Have the children help measure all the ingredients.

PROCESS

1. Mix all ingredients.
2. Mix until the dough is easy to handle.
3. If the dough is sticky, add more flour.
4. If the dough is too dry, add more water.
5. Knead the dough.
6. Roll, punch, and shape the dough as desired.
7. Bake the dough at 350 degrees for 50 to 60 minutes.

VARIATIONS

- Add food coloring to the dough for variety.
- Sprinkle colored sugar on the dough for color before baking.
- Shape the dough into letters, numbers, and shapes.

NOTES FOR NEXT TIME: _____

_____

_____

_____

Basic Clay Modeling

MATERIALS

- ☐ potter's clay (moist clay)
- ☐ plastic garbage bag
- ☐ tape
- ☐ modeling tools (plastic knives, cookie cutters, spatula, tooth-picks, spools, garlic press)

💡 HELPFUL HINT

- Notice the different ways children work with the clay. One child may pull, pinch, or squeeze the material into a desired shape. Another may make each part separately, then put them together into a whole figure. Some children may combine these two ways of working. Encourage all children in every way they work with clay.

DEVELOPMENTAL GOALS

Develop creativity, small motor development, and hand-eye coordination and explore new ways to use potter's clay.

PREPARATION

Tape down large plastic garbage bag split at the seams to cover work area. **Be sure to never have loose plastic bags around young children.**

PROCESS

1. Give each child a grapefruit-sized piece of clay.
2. Roll, pound, squeeze, pull, and press clay in any way desired.
3. Use tools to make designs, cut out clay parts, and shape in any way.
4. Leave objects to dry or place clay in airtight container to use again.

VARIATIONS

- Add sticks, tongue depressors, toothpicks, Popsicle sticks, paper clips, nails, and combs for interesting modeling tools.
- For very young clay artists, be sure tools small enough to put in the mouth are not available! All young preschoolers must be supervised in their use of clay and modeling tools.

NOTES FOR NEXT TIME: _____

_____

_____

_____

_____

Box Sculptures

MATERIALS

- ☐ boxes of different sizes and shapes
- ☐ paste
- ☐ tempera paint
- ☐ brushes
- ☐ construction paper
- ☐ scraps of fabric and trim

💡 HELPFUL HINT

- Add powdered detergent to the paint so it will stick to a wax-coated box.

DEVELOPMENTAL GOALS

Develop creativity, small motor development, and hand-eye coordination; explore a new use for a familiar object; and explore a new type of three-dimensional artwork.

PREPARATION

Have children bring in an assortment of boxes. Be sure to include cereal boxes as they make great bases for box sculpture.

PROCESS

1. Use one box as a base.
2. Glue smaller boxes on to make a sculpture design.
3. Glue on cut-construction paper details.
4. Add fabric and trim scraps for more design details.

VARIATIONS

- Make a city of box sculpture buildings.
- Paint the sculpture.
- Create box robots, imaginary animals, and anything else imagined.

NOTES FOR NEXT TIME: _____

_____

_____

_____

_____

A

All Ages

Bread-Dough Sculptures

MATERIALS

- ☐ 3 tablespoons white glue
- ☐ bread
- ☐ one or two drops of lemon juice
- ☐ paint
- ☐ brushes
- ☐ plastic bag
- ☐ mixing bowl and spoon

 **HELPFUL HINTS**

- While this is not an edible dough, some young artists may taste the dough. If this does happen, rinse the children's mouths with clear water to get rid of the pasty taste.

- Bread-dough clay can be preserved for modeling by putting it in a plastic bag and placing it in a refrigerator.

- Be sure to talk about the physical changes children will see as they make this dough!

DEVELOPMENTAL GOALS

Develop creativity, small motor development, and hand-eye coordination and explore a new form of modeling dough.

PREPARATION

Remove the crusts from four slices of bread. Tear the bread into small pieces. Children love to do this!

PROCESS

1. Mix the pieces of bread thoroughly with white glue and one or two drops of lemon juice.

2. Model or shape as desired.

3. Allow 1 or 2 days for complete drying.

VARIATIONS

- Pieces may be painted with tempera paint.
- Add details with buttons, sequins, and so on before the bread dough dries.

NOTES FOR NEXT TIME: _____

_____

_____

_____

_____

Cheerio™ Sculptures

MATERIALS

- ☐ 3 tablespoons butter
- ☐ 3 cups miniature marshmallows
- ☐ 1/2 teaspoon vanilla
- ☐ 1/2 teaspoon food coloring
- ☐ 4 cups Cheerios™
- ☐ wax paper
- ☐ large pan
- ☐ mixing spoon

💡 HELPFUL HINTS

- Be sure to cool mixture well before shaping!
- Wash the hands before mixing the recipe and before shaping the dough.
- Be sure the children stay well away from the stove during the cooking process.

DEVELOPMENTAL GOALS

Develop creativity, small motor development, and hand-eye coordination and explore a new kind of three-dimensional material.

PREPARATION

Instruct the children to wash their hands. Have the children measure all ingredients.

PROCESS

1. Melt the butter and marshmallows in a large pan over low heat.
2. Remove the mixture from the heat and add vanilla and food coloring of your choice.
3. Fold in the Cheerios™. Allow to cool.
4. Butter the hands.
5. Give each child a lump of the mixture to shape and mold on a piece of wax paper.
6. Let the sculpture set before eating.

VARIATIONS

- Separate the mixture and make two colors of sculpture dough.
- Decorate the design or shape with raisins or gumdrops.

NOTES FOR NEXT TIME: _____

_____

_____

_____

_____

3

Years Old and Up

Cinnamon Ornament Dough

MATERIALS

- ☐ 1 cup ground cinnamon
- ☐ 4 tablespoons white glue
- ☐ 3/4 cup water
- ☐ mixing bowl and spoon
- ☐ measuring cups
- ☐ cutting board
- ☐ cookie cutters
- ☐ Popsicle sticks
- ☐ straw or pencil for poking holes

 **HELPFUL HINTS**

- This is a non-edible dough. It has a very spicy, unpleasant taste.
- Unused dough can be stored in a covered container in the refrigerator for a day or two.

DEVELOPMENTAL GOALS

Develop creativity, small motor development, and hand-eye coordination; explore a new kind of play dough; and reinforce the science concepts of changing materials through mixing the dough.

PREPARATION

Have the children measure all ingredients. Discuss how each ingredient looks, feels, and tastes.

PROCESS

1. Mix all ingredients until they form a cookie-dough.
2. Add more water if the dough is too stiff.
3. Sprinkle some cinnamon on a cutting board.
4. Knead the dough on the cutting board.
5. Roll out to 1/4" thickness.
6. Use cookie cutters, Popsicle sticks, or plastic knives to cut shapes from the dough.
7. Punch a hole in the top with a straw or pencil before drying (to string a ribbon through later for hanging.)
8. Bake in 350 degree oven for 30 minutes or until firm.
9. Cool, then decorate.

VARIATIONS

- Make cinnamon-dough storybook characters. Hang them near the book corner to enjoy.
- Make name in cinnamon-dough letters. Hang them near cubby holes.
- Children can make any object they desire, not only ornaments!
- Decorate with raisins and pieces of nuts before cooking.

NOTES FOR NEXT TIME: _____

_____

Copyright © 2004, Delmar Learning **CLAY, PLAY DOUGH, AND MODELING MATERIALS** 7

Clay-Coil Pots

MATERIALS

- ☐ potter's clay
- ☐ large plastic garbage bag
- ☐ tape

 **HELPFUL HINTS**

- Older children often enjoy making "something" out of clay. This is a good activity for that purpose.
- Coil pots make nice gifts. And they are functional as well as artwork!
- Oil-based clay cannot be painted but may be exhibited when finished (away from the sun).
- Unfinished clay work may be wrapped in plastic bags or aluminum foil or placed in covered cans with child's name attached.
- Potter's clay may be painted. Use a mixture of fairly thick tempera paint so it will stick to the clay and be bright and bold in color.

DEVELOPMENTAL GOALS

Develop creativity, small motor development, and hand-eye coordination; and explore a new use for clay.

PREPARATION

Tape garbage bag split at the seams to top of work area.

PROCESS

1. Give each child a grapefruit-sized ball of potter's clay.
2. Show the child how to make snakes by rolling out pieces of clay into coils.
3. Make several coils or one very long coil.
4. Roll a small ball of clay and flatten it into a round shape for the bottom of the pot.
5. Moisten the edges of the round bottom piece with water.
6. Wrap the coils around the round bottom piece.
7. Continue wrapping the coil around and around, putting coil upon coil.
8. Moisten the pieces together as you coil.
9. Let the pot dry before painting or decorating.

VARIATIONS

- Make coils into a square-shaped box. This takes more skill and is appropriate for children over 6 years of age.
- Make free-form coil sculptures.

NOTES FOR NEXT TIME: _____

_____

Clay or Dough Crawlers

3 Years Old and Up

MATERIALS

- ☐ clay or play dough
- ☐ buttons
- ☐ pipe cleaners
- ☐ toothpicks
- ☐ sequins
- ☐ plastic
- ☐ knives
- ☐ Popsicle sticks

💡 HELPFUL HINTS

- Potter's clay can be painted when dry. Use a fairly thick tempera paint so it will stick to the clay.

- Unfinished clay work may be wrapped in plastic bags or aluminum foil or placed in covered cans with child's name attached.

- Children do not have to make insects with their clay. They can make anything that comes to mind as they work with clay.

- Have a science or picture book with pictures or insects for the children to see.

DEVELOPMENTAL GOALS

Develop creativity, small motor development, and hand-eye coordination and explore new ways to play with clay or dough.

PREPARATION

Give each child an apple-sized ball of potter's clay or play dough. Talk about bugs—real and imagined. Discuss details on bugs such as feelers, eyes, legs, etc. Have the children think about what kind of bugs they could make with clay.

PROCESS

1. Break the clay into small pieces.
2. Roll the clay into round balls for bug bodies.
3. Add pieces of pipe cleaners for feelers.
4. Toothpicks can become legs.
5. Stick on buttons for eyes.
6. Poke in sequins for other details.
7. Leave to dry.

VARIATIONS

- Make clay butterflies, caterpillars, or worms.
- Make a bug family.
- Older children can make models of insects from a science book.

NOTES FOR NEXT TIME: _____

_____

_____

_____

Clay Play with Tools

MATERIALS

- ☐ potter's clay
- ☐ rolling pins
- ☐ plastic knives
- ☐ forks
- ☐ cookie cutters
- ☐ garlic press (optional)
- ☐ wooden clay hammers
- ☐ plastic garbage bag
- ☐ tape

💡 HELPFUL HINTS

- A small lump of clay can be used as a magnet to pick up crumbs at cleanup time.
- Unfinished clay work may be wrapped in plastic bags or aluminum foil or placed in covered cans with the child's name attached.
- Oil-base clay cannot be painted but may be exhibited when finished (away from the sun).
- Some children will enjoy manipulating clay without making anything, which is acceptable. Others may want to give names to objects. Encourage all children whatever their approach to clay activities.

DEVELOPMENTAL GOALS

Develop creativity, small motor development, and hand-eye coordination and explore clay as a three-dimensional material.

PREPARATION

Cover work area with garbage bag taped to work surface.

PROCESS

1. Give each child a grapefruit-sized ball of clay.
2. Pat or roll the clay as desired.
3. Encourage the child to squeeze, pinch, or pull the clay into desired shapes.
4. Roll the clay into snakes and little balls.
5. Cut out the clay with cookie cutters or plastic knives.
6. Squeeze the clay through a garlic press.
7. Create texture using fingernails.

VARIATIONS

- For permanent clay sculptures, allow the clay shapes to dry.
- Moisten parts of the clay to join pieces of clay.

NOTES FOR NEXT TIME: _____

_____

_____

_____

Cornstarch!

MATERIALS

☐ 3 cups cornstarch

☐ 2 cups warm water

☐ mixing bowl and spoon

 **HELPFUL HINTS**

- Cornstarch works well in a baby bathtub set on a table, with a limit of two or three children making the recipe.

- This is a clean sort of play: the white, powdery mess on the floor can be cleaned easily with a dustpan and a brush or vacuum cleaner.

- Children come back to this cornstarch and water mix again and again, because it feels good and behaves in an interesting way.

DEVELOPMENTAL GOALS

Develop creativity, small motor development, and hand-eye coordination and explore a new kind of manipulative material.

PREPARATION

Have the children measure all ingredients.

PROCESS

1. Put the ingredients in a bowl and mix with the hands.

2. The mixture will solidify when left alone, but it turns to liquid from the heat of the hands. Magic!

3. Wet cornstarch forms an unstable material, which is fun because it exhibits unexpected behavior. It breaks, but it also melts.

VARIATIONS

- Rest the fingers lightly on the surface of the cornstarch-water mix. Let your fingers drift down to the bottom of the container. If you try to punch your way to the bottom, it will resist.

- Leave the cornstarch-water mixture in the container overnight. By morning it is dry. Add some water, and it becomes that wonderful "stuff" again. Be sure to invite the children to watch this event!

NOTES FOR NEXT TIME: _____

_____

_____

_____

_____

Creative Clay

MATERIALS

- ☐ 1 cup cornstarch
- ☐ 2 cups baking soda (1-pound package)
- ☐ 1-1/4 cups cold water
- ☐ measuring cups
- ☐ mixing bowl and spoon
- ☐ plate
- ☐ damp cloth

💡 HELPFUL HINTS

- Creative clay dries at room temperature in about 3 days.
- It can be dried in a 200 degree oven.
- Use the clay immediately or store it in an air-tight container.
- Be sure the children are well away from the heat source during this activity!

DEVELOPMENTAL GOALS

Develop creativity, small motor development, and hand-eye coordination; explore a new modeling material; and reinforce the science concepts of changing materials through making the recipe.

PREPARATION

Have the children measure all ingredients. Talk about how each looks, feels, tastes, and smells.

PROCESS

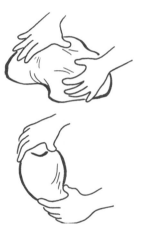

1. Stir the starch and soda together.
2. Mix in cold water.
3. Stir over medium heat until the mixture has the consistency of mashed potatoes.
4. Turn the mixture onto a plate and cover it with a damp cloth until cool enough to handle.
5. Knead when cool enough to touch.

VARIATIONS

- Add food coloring for colored clay.
- This clay has a smooth consistency and is great for modeling or making ornaments or even pottery.
- Cut out creative clay with cookie cutters.
- Cut out numbers and letters from creative clay.

NOTES FOR NEXT TIME: _____

_____

_____

_____

Crepe-Paper Clay

MATERIALS

- ☐ crepe paper
- ☐ 1 cup flour
- ☐ 1 cup salt
- ☐ large container
- ☐ water

HELPFUL HINTS

- It is best to use one color of crepe paper at a time to produce a clear solid color clay. Crepe paper colors do not mix well.
- Store crepe paper clay in a covered container in the refrigerator.

DEVELOPMENTAL GOALS

Develop creativity, small motor development, and hand-eye coordination; explore a new use for a familiar material; and explore a new kind of modeling material.

PREPARATION

Place crepe paper in a large container and add enough water to cover the paper. Soak for about 1 hour until most of water absorbs into the paper.

PROCESS

1. Pour off excess water.
2. Add small amounts of flour and salt until mixture is clay-like.
3. Mold and form shapes by hand with crepe paper clay.
4. Let the forms dry.

VARIATIONS

- Apply a clear coat of varnish to dried forms to seal.
- Apply a mixture of glue and water to seal the crepe paper clay forms.

NOTES FOR NEXT TIME: _____

_____

_____

_____

4

Years Old and Up

Cube Sculptures

MATERIALS

- ☐ boxes of sugar cubes
- ☐ white craft glue
- ☐ toothpicks
- ☐ scrap pieces of fabric and trim
- ☐ beads
- ☐ buttons
- ☐ construction paper

💡 HELPFUL HINTS

- You will probably have a lot of tasting experiences in this activity. Be sure children wash their hands before the activity and keep the tasting experiences to their own artwork!

- Because sugar cubes are small, this activity is most appropriate for children who have fairly good small muscle development in their fingers and hands. It is not easy for very young children to manipulate an item as small as a sugar cube.

- The 2s and 3s may confuse the edible sugar cube with the nonedible glue. For this reason, this activity is not recommended for this age group.

DEVELOPMENTAL GOALS

Develop creativity, small motor development, and hand-eye coordination; and explore new kinds of three-dimensional materials.

PREPARATION

Give each child a good supply of sugar cubes.

PROCESS

1. Glue the sugar cubes together to make forms and shapes.

2. Add details by gluing on buttons, pieces of trim, beads, and so on.

3. Glue the cube sculpture to a construction paper base for display.

VARIATIONS

- Include marshmallows in the cube sculpture.
- Add flavoring such as lemon or maple extract to some sugar cubes. Let them dry and harden before using in this activity.

NOTES FOR NEXT TIME: _____

_____

_____

_____

A
All Ages

Easy Dough

MATERIALS

- ☐ 1 cup flour
- ☐ 1 cup salt
- ☐ 1 tablespoon salad oil
- ☐ food coloring
- ☐ water
- ☐ mixing bowl and spoon
- ☐ measuring cups

 **HELPFUL HINTS**

- Because this is such an easy recipe, older children may be able to make it themselves after the first couple of tries.

- Because of the very pliable nature of easy dough, it is a great material for young children just beginning to work with clay.

DEVELOPMENTAL GOALS

Develop creativity, small motor development, and hand-eye coordination; explore a new kind of play dough; and reinforce the science concepts of changing materials through making the dough.

PREPARATION

Have the children measure all ingredients.

PROCESS

1. Mix the flour and salt.
2. Add oil.
3. Slowly add water until the mixture is pliable.
4. The dough will be spongy and clay-like.

VARIATIONS

- Add food coloring for colored easy dough.
- Divide the dough and make two colors of dough.
- Add lemon or vanilla extract for a nice smell.
- Add cinnamon or clove powder for another pleasant smell.

NOTES FOR NEXT TIME: _____

_____

_____

_____

_____

Easy Fudge Dough

MATERIALS

- ☐ 1/4 cup butter
- ☐ 1/4 cup sweet-ened condensed milk
- ☐ 1 teaspoon vanilla
- ☐ 1 pound confec-tioner's sugar
- ☐ 3/4 cup cocoa
- ☐ 1/4 teaspoon salt
- ☐ mixing bowl and spoon
- ☐ measuring cups and spoons
- ☐ wax paper

💡 HELPFUL HINTS

- Wrap a few pieces in aluminum foil for a nice gift for special occasions.
- Be sure to keep children a safe distance from the stove during the cooking part of the recipe.
- Remember to point out the changes in materials when they are mixed.

DEVELOPMENTAL GOALS

Develop creativity, small motor development, and hand-eye coordination; explore a new kind of modeling material and reinforce the science concept of material as it changes during mixing.

PREPARATION

Instruct the children to wash their hands. Have the children help measure all ingredients. Talk about the look, feel, smell, and taste of each ingredient.

PROCESS

1. Melt the butter in a saucepan or in the microwave for 10 seconds on high.
2. Stir in the milk and vanilla.
3. Gradually add the mixture of sugar, cocoa, and salt.
4. Mix until soft and creamy.
5. Give each child a spoonful of fudge to mold with the hands.
6. Put the molded fudge on a piece of wax paper and chill.
7. Eat and enjoy!

VARIATIONS

- Use Popsicle sticks to cut and shape the fudge.
- Press the fudge into a buttered pan. Chill and cut into squares.
- For children over 3, top each piece with a piece of walnut or pecan half.
- Do not use nuts if any child has a food allergy.

NOTES FOR NEXT TIME: _____

_____

_____

_____

A
All Ages

Favorite Play Dough

MATERIALS

- ☐ 2 cups flour
- ☐ 1 cup salt
- ☐ 4 teaspoons cream of tartar
- ☐ 2 cups water
- ☐ 2 tablespoons salad oil
- ☐ food coloring
- ☐ measuring spoons and cups
- ☐ pot
- ☐ mixing spoon

 **HELPFUL HINTS**

- Dough can be frozen and refrozen several times.
- Be very careful that children stand well away from the stove during the cooking process.

DEVELOPMENTAL GOALS

Develop creativity, small motor development, and hand-eye coordination; explore a new kind of play dough; and reinforce the science concepts of changing materials.

PREPARATION

Have children measure all ingredients. Talk about how each ingredient looks, feels, smells, and tastes.

PROCESS

1. Mix all ingredients in a pot.
2. Cook over medium heat until soft, lumpy ball forms. It happens quickly!
3. Knead for a few minutes until the dough is smooth.
4. Store in an airtight container.

VARIATIONS

- Add food coloring for colored play dough.
- Add spices and extracts such as cinnamon and lemon extract for a yummy-smelling play dough.

NOTES FOR NEXT TIME: _____

_____

_____

_____

3
Years Old and UP

Feather and Pipe-Cleaner Sculptures

MATERIALS

☐ small paper plates
☐ play dough
☐ feathers
☐ pipe cleaners
☐ beads
☐ doughnut-shaped cereal (Cheerios™)

💡 **HELPFUL HINTS**

- You may have to show the children how to make spirals with the pipe cleaners. Give a simple demonstration, then let the children do it themselves.

- Do the same with threading beads or cereal on the pipe cleaners. Give one demonstration, then let the children experiment.

- Have a good supply of doughnut-shaped cereal on hand. Little artists get hungry!

- With 2s and 3s, do not mix beads with cereal pieces, because they are choking hazards.

- If you lack enough feathers for this activity, the pipe cleaners and cereal work well without them.

DEVELOPMENTAL GOALS

Develop creativity, small motor development, and hand-eye coordination and explore a new kind of three-dimensional sculpture.

PREPARATION

Give each child a small paper plate containing a ball of play dough about the size of a golf ball.

PROCESS

1. Flatten the ball just a bit.
2. Wrap the pipe cleaners around pencils or the children's fingers to make spirals.
3. Thread the beads or cereal pieces onto the pipe cleaners.
4. Stick the feathers and pipe cleaners into the play dough.

VARIATION

- Add other details, such as twigs, dried weeds, flowers, or buttons.

NOTES FOR NEXT TIME: _____

_____

_____

_____

Foil Sculptures

MATERIALS

- ☐ foil
- ☐ gummed or transparent tape
- ☐ brush
- ☐ liquid detergent
- ☐ tempera paint
- ☐ cardboard
- ☐ paintbrushes
- ☐ tacky glue

💡 HELPFUL HINTS

- This is a good activity for recycling aluminum foil.
- An adult may help attach the foil sculpture to the cardboard base with a glue gun.

DEVELOPMENTAL GOALS

Develop creativity, small motor development, and hand-eye coordination and explore a new use of foil as a three-dimensional material.

PREPARATION

Crumple the foil into all kinds of forms.

PROCESS

1. Use pieces of crumpled foil to create an object or a design.
2. Join these forms with tape or tacky glue.
3. Glue the forms to a piece of cardboard for a base.
4. After the glue sets, paint the forms with a drop or two of liquid detergent mixed in tempera paint.

VARIATIONS

- Add fabric and trim scraps, feathers, and buttons for fun details.
- Create foil animals, flowers, trees, or even people!

NOTES FOR NEXT TIME: _____

_____

_____

_____

_____

Fun Decorations

MATERIALS

- ☐ play clay (see recipe on page 34)
- ☐ rolling pin
- ☐ cookie cutters of all sizes
- ☐ bottle tops
- ☐ plastic knife
- ☐ needle
- ☐ string or yarn
- ☐ wax paper

 **HELPFUL HINTS**

- Play clay may take up to 36 hours to dry. Be sure to store the drying objects in a safe place away from accidents!

- To speed drying, heat the oven to 350 degrees, then turn the oven off and place the objects on a wire rack or in a cardboard box on the rack. Leave in the oven until the oven is cool.

DEVELOPMENTAL GOALS

Develop creativity, small motor development, and hand-eye coordination; explore a new kind of play dough; and reinforce the science concept of change in materials while mixing the dough.

PREPARATION

Make play clay using the "Play Clay" recipe in this book. Let the children measure and mix the ingredients. Talk about the physical changes in materials when wet and dry materials are mixed.

PROCESS

1. Roll out the play clay to 1/4 inch thickness on wax paper.

2. Cut out shapes with cookie cutters.

3. Cut out free-form shapes, too.

4. Poke a hole in the top of the cut-out object.

5. Let the object dry before inserting yarn in the hole.

VARIATIONS

- Objects may be left white or painted when dry.
- Sprinkle with glitter when the play clay is wet for a glittery effect.

NOTES FOR NEXT TIME: _____

_____

_____

_____

A

All Ages

Gloop

MATERIALS

- ☐ 8 oz. white craft glue
- ☐ 1 cup water
- ☐ 1 cup warm water
- ☐ 1-1/2 teaspoon borax powder
- ☐ tempera paint
- ☐ one large and one small mixing bowl
- ☐ spoon
- ☐ measuring cups and spoons

💡 HELPFUL HINTS

- Elmer's Glue™ works well in this recipe.
- Store the gloop in an airtight container.
- Gloop is very much like silly putty—stretchy and fun to play with!
- Press gloop over colored comic strips. Then, press the gloop on a piece of paper to make a print of the drawing.

DEVELOPMENTAL GOALS

Develop creativity, small motor development, and hand-eye coordination and explore a new kind of modeling material.

PREPARATION

Have the children measure all ingredients. Talk about how each material looks, feels, and smells.

PROCESS

1. Pour the glue into a large bowl.
2. Add water and stir until blended.
3. Add a few drops of paint and stir until mixed well.
4. Set this mixture aside.
5. In a small bowl, stir together the warm water and borax powder until the powder dissolves.
6. Slowly pour this mixture into the glue mixture, stirring constantly for 2 minutes.
7. Knead the mixture with the hands until it is smooth and stretchy.

VARIATION

- Leave out the tempera paint and make white gloop.

NOTES FOR NEXT TIME: _____

_____

_____

_____

CLAY, PLAY DOUGH, AND MODELING MATERIALS

Homemade Glitter Clay

MATERIALS

- ☐ 3 cups flour
- ☐ 1-1/2 cups salt
- ☐ 6 teaspoons cream of tartar
- ☐ 4 tablespoons vegetable oil
- ☐ 3 cups water
- ☐ food coloring
- ☐ glitter (you will need at least 5 containers)
- ☐ large pot
- ☐ mixing spoon
- ☐ measuring cups and spoons

 **HELPFUL HINTS**

- This clay is very salty. Do not let children eat it!
- Be sure children stay well away from the stove top during the cooking process.
- When not in use, store the glitter clay in a plastic bag or plastic container.

DEVELOPMENTAL GOALS

Develop creativity, small motor development, and hand-eye coordination and explore a new kind of play dough.

PREPARATION

Let the children measure all the ingredients.

PROCESS

1. In a pot, combine the flour, salt, and cream of tartar.
2. Add the oil, water, and food coloring.
3. Mix until there are no lumps and the color is uniform.
4. Have adult heat the mixture on medium heat, stirring constantly.
5. Heat the mixture until it forms a ball and pulls away from the sides of the pan.
6. Let the mixture cool.
7. Have the children knead the glitter into the clay by flattening the clay with the hands and pouring some glitter on it. Fold over the clay and knead it for a while.
8. Repeat until the clay looks glittery.
9. Use glitter clay to mold objects and designs.

VARIATIONS

- Make two colors of glitter dough.
- Make glitter dough numbers, letters, and ornaments.

NOTES FOR NEXT TIME: _____

_____

Honey Dough

MATERIALS

- ☐ 3 tablespoons honey
- ☐ 4 tablespoons peanut butter
- ☐ 1/2 cup nonfat dry milk
- ☐ 1/4 cup dry cereal flakes (crushed)
- ☐ mixing bowl and spoon
- ☐ measuring cups and spoons
- ☐ wax paper
- ☐ butter or margarine

💡 HELPFUL HINTS

- This recipe makes 18 1" balls.
- Be sure the children wash their hands well before mixing the recipe and again before shaping the honey dough.
- Always be sure to check for peanut allergies before using any edible-dough recipe with peanuts or peanut butter.

DEVELOPMENTAL GOALS

Develop creativity, small motor development, and hand-eye coordination; explore a new kind of play dough, relate the science concepts of changing materials to art activities.

PREPARATION

Instruct the children to wash their hands. Have the children measure all ingredients and crush the cereal flakes with a spoon on wax paper. Talk about the appearance, color, taste, and texture of each of the ingredients.

PROCESS

1. Mix the honey and peanut butter in a bowl.
2. Gradually add the nonfat dry milk. Mix well.
3. Give each child a pat of butter or margarine to grease the hands.

4. Give each child a lump of dough to shape into balls or any other desired form.
5. Roll the balls or shapes in dry cereal flakes.
6. Chill until firm.

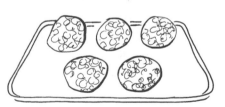

VARIATIONS

- Roll honey-dough balls in graham cracker crumbs.
- Shape the dough in numbers or letters.
- A group of children can make the letters for a sign or a title for a party or special group project.

NOTES FOR NEXT TIME: _____

_____

_____

_____

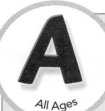

A
All Ages

Kool-Aid™ Play Dough

MATERIALS

- ☐ 2-1/2 cup flour
- ☐ 1/2 cup salt
- ☐ 2 packages unsweetened Kool-Aid™
- ☐ 2 cups boiling water
- ☐ 3 tablespoons vegetable oil
- ☐ measuring cups and spoons
- ☐ mixing bowl and spoon

HELPFUL HINTS

- This recipe lasts for several months stored in an air-tight container between uses.
- Children will enjoy this different use of a familiar drink mix.
- Be sure to talk about how the ingredients change while they are being mixed.

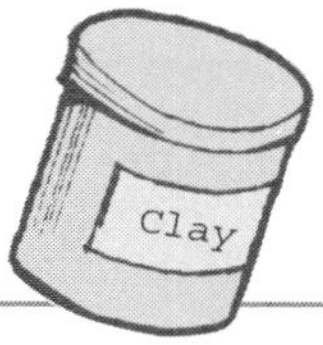

DEVELOPMENTAL GOALS

Develop creativity, small motor development, and hand-eye coordination; explore a new kind of play dough; and reinforce the science concept of changing materials through mixing the dough.

PREPARATION

Have the children measure all ingredients.

PROCESS

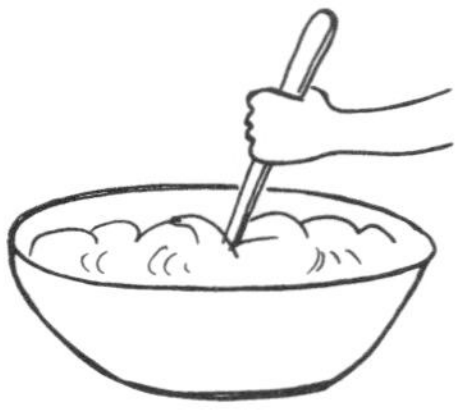

1. Mix all dry ingredients.
2. Add water and oil and stir.
3. Knead with the hands when the mixture is cool.
4. Store the dough in an air-tight container.

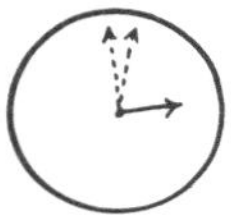

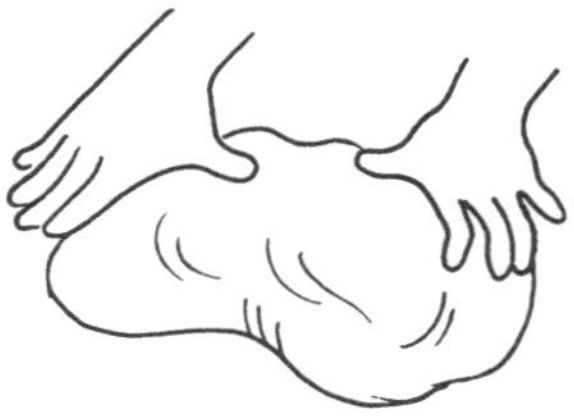

VARIATIONS

- Mix dough in colors for holidays or special occasions.
- Add spices or extracts such as lemon, vanilla, and cinnamon for fun smells.

NOTES FOR NEXT TIME: ______________________________

____

____

____

Marshmallow Sculptures

MATERIALS

- ☐ Styrofoam plates or trays
- ☐ miniature and regular sized marshmallows
- ☐ toothpicks
- ☐ gum drops
- ☐ pieces of vegetables
- ☐ grapes

 **HELPFUL HINT**

- Be sure to have a good supply of marshmallows on hand for this activity. Little artists get hungry!

DEVELOPMENTAL GOALS

Develop creativity, small motor development, and hand-eye coordination; explore a new modeling material; and practice three-dimensional designs.

PREPARATION

Instruct the children to wash their hands. Cut up gum drops, grapes, and vegetables into small pieces.

PROCESS

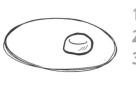

1. Give each child a Styrofoam plate.
2. Use one marshmallow as the base.
3. Build a sculpture with other marshmallows and toothpicks.
4. Add details with bits of gumdrops, grapes, and vegetable pieces.

VARIATIONS

- Use colored marshmallows and regular white marshmallows.
- Make marshmallow animals, people, trees, flowers, and so on.
- Make marshmallow decorations for a special occasion.

NOTES FOR NEXT TIME: _____

_____

_____

_____

Mary's Dough

MATERIALS

- ☐ 1 egg
- ☐ 1-1/2 cups warm water
- ☐ 1 package yeast
- ☐ 1 teaspoon salt
- ☐ 1 tablespoon sugar
- ☐ 4 cups flour
- ☐ measuring cups and spoons
- ☐ large bowl
- ☐ mixing spoon
- ☐ cookie sheet
- ☐ grease
- ☐ pastry brush

 HELPFUL HINTS

- Be very careful that children do not stand too near the stove.

- Be sure to include such vocabulary words as *liquid*, *solids*, and *tart* when mixing play dough.

- Because this dough uses very little sugar, it is a healthy alternative to most cookie doughs.

DEVELOPMENTAL GOALS

Develop creativity, small motor development, and hand-eye coordination; explore a new kind of play dough; and reinforce the idea of changing materials when mixing the dough.

PREPARATION

Instruct the children to wash their hands. Have the children help measure and pour the ingredients into the bowl and mix. Talk about how materials look different when they are mixed. Let the children taste each of the ingredients. Talk about the tastes and how they differ.

PROCESS

1. Pour 1-1/2 cups warm water into the bowl.
2. Sprinkle the yeast into the water and stir until it is dissolved.
3. Add salt, sugar, and flour. Mix together to form a ball.
4. Sprinkle flour onto the work surface and place dough on it.
5. Let the children knead the dough until it is smooth and elastic.
6. Encourage the children to roll and twist the dough into shapes.
7. Place the dough sculptures on the cookie sheet and cover it with a clean towel. Place in warm area to rise.
8. After dough designs have doubled in size, brush each one with a beaten egg.
9. Cook dough in 350-degree oven for 12 to 15 minutes until they are firm and golden brown.
10. Remove from oven, cool, and enjoy!

VARIATIONS

- Sprinkle sugar or salt on shapes before baking.
- Make dough letters, numbers, animals, or people.

NOTES FOR NEXT TIME: _____

_____

Mobile Sculptures

4 Years Old and Up

MATERIALS

- ☐ tree branches
- ☐ string
- ☐ natural objects such as leaves, acorns, pinecones
- ☐ construction paper
- ☐ wax paper

HELPFUL HINTS

- If the waxed paper does not stay attached to the leaves, the wax coating left by the heat application is enough to harden and preserve the leaves.
- Children may watch the ironing process, but it must be done by an adult. And children need to be closely supervised during the process.
- Adult may need to help child knot the string.
- An adult may need to help the child attach the string so the branch hangs horizontally. This is a good experiment in balance!
- This activity is most appropriate for children with good small motor development.

DEVELOPMENTAL GOALS

Develop creativity, small motor development, and hand-eye coordination; and explore a new three-dimensional activity.

PREPARATION

Go on an outdoor walk with the children. Instruct each child to find a branch about 12 inches long to use in this activity. Collect leaves and other items as well.

PROCESS

1. Adult presses the leaves between two sheets of wax paper, using an iron on the "low" setting. This preserves the leaves.
2. When the wax paper has cooled, cut around the leaves to separate them for the mobile.
3. Adult makes holes in the leaves with a blunt needle, hairpin, or pencil point.
4. Insert string or thin yarn into the holes in each of the leaves. Knot the string or yarn.
5. Attach a piece of string or yarn (about 12 inches long) to the branch, so that the branch hangs horizontally.
6. Tie the leaves on the branch in various places.
7. Leaf shapes cut out of red, yellow, orange and brown construction paper can also be attached to the branch with yarn.
8. Acorns, pinecones and berries may also be strung and attached for added color and variety.

VARIATIONS

- Make theme mobiles such as "All about Me" with cut-out pictures of favorite things.
- Make mobiles of "My Family" or "My Friends."
- Make mobiles with favorite storybook characters.

NOTES FOR NEXT TIME: _____

_____

A

Mud Bricks

DEVELOPMENTAL GOALS

Develop creativity, small motor development, and hand-eye coordination and explore a new clay technique.

PREPARATION

Dig up dirt outdoors. This is a fun thing for children to do, so you will not lack the dirt you need!

MATERIALS

- ☐ dirt
- ☐ warm area or oven
- ☐ muffin tins
- ☐ plastic bucket
- ☐ newspaper
- ☐ mixing spoon

💡 **HELPFUL HINT**

- Children usually love playing in the mud. Be prepared for a lot of side activities besides making bricks! Enjoy the slippery, cool feel of the mud yourself, too!

PROCESS

1. Put the dirt in the bucket.
2. Make mud by mixing in a little water at a time.
3. Make it a thick mud.
4. Press the mud into muffin tin cups.
5. It takes about 10 days to set, or bake at 250 degrees for 15 minutes.
6. Spread newspaper on the floor.
7. Create a design using mud bricks.

VARIATIONS

- Add plaster of paris to the mud mixture to help it stick together better.
- Add pieces of twigs, stones, and bits of wood to the design.
- Dig up dirt from different areas of soil. Compare the colors, feel, and texture. Talk about how different the bricks look from each type of soil.

NOTES FOR NEXT TIME: _____

_____

Clay

Natural Object Sculptures

MATERIALS

- ☐ clay or play dough
- ☐ natural objects of various sizes and colors (e.g., seeds, twigs, pine cones, seed pods, stones, driftwood, leaves)
- ☐ quick-drying glue
- ☐ construction paper
- ☐ felt
- ☐ fabric and trim scraps

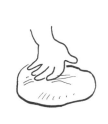 **HELPFUL HINTS**

- Encourage the children to arrange and rearrange the objects until they are satisfied with the sculpture before gluing it down.
- The younger the child, the shorter the attention span, so expect that very young children will probably use only a few items for this sculpture activity.
- Older children will enjoy adding more details. Be prepared with a wider variety of materials for this age group.

DEVELOPMENTAL GOALS

Develop creativity, small motor development, and hand-eye coordination; explore a new three-dimensional technique; and relate science to art activities.

PREPARATION

Talk about the collection of natural items. Discuss how they can be put together to make a design. Include a discussion on the lines, shapes, sizes, and other details of the natural objects.

PROCESS

1. Use a lump of play dough as a base.
2. Flatten the lump for the base.
3. Poke several natural items into the dough base.
4. When satisfied with the creation, leave it to dry.

VARIATIONS

- Paint or colored paper can be added to enhance the sculpture.
- Use a piece of driftwood or a large twig as the base. Glue objects to it.
- Use toothpicks to attach other interesting items, such as buttons or sequins.

NOTES FOR NEXT TIME: _____

_____

_____

_____

_____

A

Ornamental Dough

MATERIALS

- ☐ 1 cup cornstarch
- ☐ 1-1/4 cups water
- ☐ 2 cups baking soda
- ☐ measuring cups
- ☐ spoon for stirring
- ☐ cooking pot (double boiler/ optional)

 **HELPFUL HINTS**

- This activity is suitable for dried objects.
- Let the children measure all ingredients.
- Be very careful with children around the hot stove and pan.
- This dough does not store well. It is best used for making dried objects.
- This dough does not taste good, but it will not harm the children if they taste it.

DEVELOPMENTAL GOALS

Develop creativity, small motor development, and hand-eye coordination; explore a new kind of play dough; and reinforce the science concepts of change in materials while mixing the dough.

PREPARATION

Have the children help measure the ingredients. Mix the ingredients in a pan. Discuss how different the materials look when they are dry and when they are wet and mixed. Use such proper measuring terms such as 1 *cup*. Talk about how materials taste, too.

PROCESS

1. An adult cooks the ingredients until thickened, either in a double boiler or over direct heat. Stir constantly.
2. Cool the mixure.
3. Have the children knead the dough.
4. Have the children make dough into whatever they wish.
5. If the dough is to be used for ornaments, make a hole for hanging the ornament while the dough is still moist.

VARIATIONS

- Add dry tempera paint for vivid colors.
- Sprinkle glitter on wet dough objects for a shiny effect.

NOTES FOR NEXT TIME: _____

_____

_____

_____

3
Years Old and UP

Painted-Clay Sculptures

MATERIALS

- ☐ non–oil-based clay (potter's clay), sometimes called "moist clay"
- ☐ rolling pin
- ☐ plastic knives
- ☐ tools such as spatula, cookie cutters, garlic press, forks
- ☐ tempera paint
- ☐ brushes
- ☐ clear gloss enamel (optional)
- ☐ plastic garbage bag
- ☐ tape

💡 HELPFUL HINT

- After the paint is dry, an adult may apply clear gloss over the clay creation for a shiny effect.
- Store the clay in an airtight container.

DEVELOPMENTAL GOALS

Develop creativity, small motor development, and hand-eye coordination and explore new ways to use clay.

PREPARATION

Tape garbage bag to top of work area.

PROCESS

1. Give each child a grape-fruit-sized ball of moist clay.
2. Roll out the clay with a rolling pin.
3. Roll out to about 1/2" thick.
4. Cut out shapes with cookie cutters.
5. Alternatively, cut out shapes with plastic knives.
6. Allow the clay design to dry.
7. Paint the designs with tempera paint.

VARIATIONS

- Add buttons, tiny stones, sequins, and other decorative details.
- Older children can create a group of clay characters, animals, or people to illustrate a favorite story or character.
- Make clay letters and numbers.

NOTES FOR NEXT TIME: _____

_____

_____

_____

Paper-Pulp Sculptures

MATERIALS

- ☐ newspaper
- ☐ powder wallpaper paste
- ☐ wintergreen oil
- ☐ bowl
- ☐ wax paper

💡 HELPFUL HINTS

- Let the children tear up the newspaper for this activity. They will love it, and it is good exercise for the small muscles in the fingers and hands.
- Dried paper-pulp objects can be painted with tempera paint or decorated with markers.

DEVELOPMENTAL GOALS

Develop creativity, small motor development, and hand-eye coordination and explore a new three-dimensional material.

PREPARATION

Tear newspaper into tiny pieces and strips. Soak overnight in water.

PROCESS

1. Squeeze excess water from the newspaper pieces.
2. Add powder wallpaper paste and few drops of oil of wintergreen to prevent mold.
3. Keep adding wallpaper paste until a doughy consistency is reached.
4. Knead the mixture until it is smooth and pliable.
5. Mold into shapes or designs on piece of wax paper.
6. Let dry for several days before painting.

VARIATIONS

- Add food coloring to the mixture for colored paper pulp.
- Use buttons, beads, pinecones, and tiny stones for added details. Poke them into the wet paper pulp before drying.

NOTES FOR NEXT TIME: _____

_____

_____

_____

Peanut-Butter No-Cook Dough

MATERIALS

- ☐ mixing bowl and spoon
- ☐ 1 cup peanut butter
- ☐ 1 cup Karo® syrup
- ☐ 1-1/4 cups nonfat dry milk solids
- ☐ 1 cup sifted confectioner's sugar

 **HELPFUL HINTS**

- Be sure the children wash their hands well before this activity, as well as before shaping their peanut-butter objects—especially if they will be eating them later!

- If the dough is too sticky, add more dry milk.

- Always be sure that the children are not allergic to peanuts before conducting this activity.

DEVELOPMENTAL GOALS

Develop creativity, small motor development, and hand-eye coordination; explore a new type of play dough; and reinforce science concepts through mixing of materials.

PREPARATION

Instruct the children to wash their hands. Have the children sift the confectioner's sugar and measure all ingredients. Discuss each of the materials, its texture, its appearance, and its taste.

PROCESS

1. Blend the peanut butter and syrup in a large mixing bowl.

2. Mix the dry milk and sifted confectioner's sugar.

3. Mix all ingredients—first with a spoon, then with the hands.

4. Turn the mixture onto board and continue kneading until the mixture is well blended and smooth.

5. Give the child a ball of dough to knead and shape.

6. To make cut-out cookies, roll the dough to 1/2" thickness.

VARIATIONS

- Top the mixture with raisins or nuts.
- Make peanut-butter animals to eat at snack time.

NOTES FOR NEXT TIME: _____

_____

_____

_____

3 Years Old and UP

Play Clay

MATERIALS

- ☐ 1 cup cornstarch
- ☐ 2 cups baking soda (1-pound package)
- ☐ 1-1/4 cups water
- ☐ saucepan
- ☐ measuring cups
- ☐ spoon

 **HELPFUL HINTS**

- For solid-colored play clay, add a few drops of food coloring or tempera paint powder to water before it is mixed with the starch and soda.

- Be sure to talk about the physical changes the children can see during the mixing and making of the dough.

- Be ever watchful of children when working at the stove. Adult supervision must be constant when at the stove.

DEVELOPMENTAL GOALS

Develop creativity, small motor development, and hand-eye coordination; explore a new kind of dough; and reinforce the science concept of change in materials during mixing.

PREPARATION

Let the children measure all ingredients.

PROCESS

1. Mix the cornstarch and baking soda thoroughly in a saucepan.

2. Mix in water.

3. Bring to a boil over medium heat, stirring constantly, until the mixture reaches a moist, mashed-potato consistency.

4. Remove the mixture immediately from heat.

5. Turn the mixture out on a plate and cover it with a damp cloth until cool.

6. When the mixture is easy to handle, the children can knead it like dough.

7. Shape the clay as desired or store it in a tightly closed plastic bag for later use.

VARIATIONS

- Objects may be left white or painted when dry.

- Sprinkle glitter onto the wet play clay. The object will dry even more sparkly!

- Play clay can be shaped into small balls or ovals for beads. Have a adult use a long pin or needle to make a hole for string or yarn to hang the ornament.

NOTES FOR NEXT TIME: _____

_____

34 **CLAY, PLAY DOUGH, AND MODELING MATERIALS** Copyright © 2004, Delmar Learning

Play Clay Pins and Buttons

MATERIALS

- ☐ play clay (see the preceding "Play Clay" activity)
- ☐ rolling pin
- ☐ plastic knife
- ☐ tempera paint
- ☐ sparkle
- ☐ glue
- ☐ wax paper
- ☐ blunt-tipped needle

💡 HELPFUL HINTS

- Dough thicker than 1/4" will make the objects too heavy to wear.
- Play-clay objects will dry and harden at room temperature in approximately 36 hours, depending on thickness.
- To speed drying, heat the oven to 350 degrees. Turn the oven off and place the objects on a wire rack or in a cardboard box on the rack. Leave the play clay in the oven until the oven is cool.

DEVELOPMENTAL GOALS

Develop creativity, small motor development, and hand-eye coordination; explore a new use for play dough; and reinforce the design concepts of line, pattern, and balance.

PREPARATION

Prepare play clay according to the "Play Clay" activity in this book. Let the children measure and mix the ingredients.

PROCESS

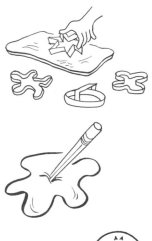

1. Roll out the play clay to 1/4 inch thickness on wax paper.
2. Cut the play clay into circles or other designs.
3. Moisten each piece slightly so the pieces stick together.
4. Alternatively, glue the pieces in place when dry.
5. Use the blunt-tipped needle to make holes for buttons. For pins, glue a safety pin to the back when dry.

VARIATIONS

- Paint pins and buttons with tempera paint after the play clay has dried.
- Sprinkle on glitter before drying for a sparkly effect.
- Dried play clay can be decorated with felt-tip markers.
- Dry play clay can also be sprayed with clear plastic, dipped into shellac, or coated with clear nail polish for a permanent finish. Be sure to use any spray in a well-ventilated area!

NOTES FOR NEXT TIME: _____

_____

Play Dough Beads and Such

MATERIALS

- ☐ 1/2 cup flour
- ☐ 1/3 cup cornstarch
- ☐ 1/2 cup salt
- ☐ 1/3 cup warm water
- ☐ mixing bowl and spoon
- ☐ measuring cups
- ☐ paint
- ☐ paint brushes
- ☐ thread
- ☐ needle

💡 HELPFUL HINTS

- To dry beads, stick toothpicks into a ball of play dough. Then, place a bead on each toothpick.
- As the beads dry, twist the beads on the toothpicks to keep them from sticking to the toothpicks.
- Children can make any other kind of object with the dough if they are not interested in making beads.

DEVELOPMENTAL GOALS

Develop creativity, small motor development, and hand-eye coordination and explore a new kind of modeling material.

PREPARATION

Have the children measure all ingredients.

PROCESS

1. Mix the dry ingredients.
2. Add warm water gradually until the mixture can be kneaded into a stiff dough.
3. If the dough is sticky, dust it with dry flour.
4. Roll the play clay into 1/2-inch balls.
5. Make holes in the balls with toothpick.
6. When dry, paint the beads and string on thread.

VARIATIONS

- Add food coloring or dry tempera paint to the dough for colored play-dough beads.
- Roll out the dough and cut out shapes with cookie cutters. Make a hole in the top for hanging.
- Encourage the children to make original shapes and designs with the dough.

NOTES FOR NEXT TIME: _____
_____
_____

Years Old and Up

Play Dough Seed Collage

MATERIALS

- [ ] ball of play dough or clay
- [ ] plastic lids
- [ ] seeds, beans, other grains

💡 HELPFUL HINTS

- These dough objects do not have to be left to dry. They can be disassembled, if preferred.
- Clay works well with this activity, as well.
- Talk about what a pattern is: repeating a shape or design. Discuss how a pattern can be used in this activity.
- Introduce the idea of contrast: how different things can be placed near each other to make them stand out. For example, discuss placing a large, shiny stone next to a small, green one.

DEVELOPMENTAL GOALS

Develop creativity, small motor development, and hand-eye coordination; explore a new use for play dough; and practice such design concepts as balance, line, and pattern.

PREPARATION

Give each child a ball of play dough large enough to fit inside the plastic lid.

PROCESS

1. Roll the play dough into a ball.
2. Press the dough into the plastic lid.
3. Arrange seeds, beans, and other grains on the dough.
4. Press the materials into the dough.
5. Allow the dough to dry.

VARIATIONS

- Add other details, such as feathers, small stones, and twigs.
- Press an assortment of buttons into the play dough.

NOTES FOR NEXT TIME: _____

_____

_____

_____

Potato Dough

MATERIALS

- ☐ 1/3 cup mashed potatoes
- ☐ 1-3/4 cups powdered sugar
- ☐ 1 teaspoon vanilla
- ☐ 2 cups flaked coconut
- ☐ measuring cups and spoons
- ☐ mixing bowl and spoon

💡 HELPFUL HINTS

- Be sure the children wash their hands before mixing the recipe and again before shaping the dough.

- This is a fun recipe for young children, because it uses something they think of as a vegetable in a sweet way!

- Because this activity involves no heating, it is a good recipe for very young cooking-artists. It is edible, too!

DEVELOPMENTAL GOALS

Develop creativity, small motor development, and hand-eye coordination and explore a new kind of play dough.

PREPARATION

Instruct children to wash their hands. Prepare the mashed potatoes, either from potatoes or from dry, flaked potatoes. Have the children measure all ingredients.

PROCESS

1. Mix the ingredients in a bowl thoroughly.
2. Give each child a lump of potato dough on a piece of wax paper.
3. Shape the dough into desired shapes.
4. Place the dough in the refrigerator until very cool.

VARIATIONS

- Add details with bits of raisins, nuts, or semisweet chocolate pieces.
- Shape the dough into numbers or letters.

NOTES FOR NEXT TIME: _____

_____

_____

_____

Rock Sculptures

MATERIALS

- ☐ rocks of various sizes
- ☐ glue
- ☐ markers
- ☐ paint
- ☐ scraps of fabric, trim

💡 HELPFUL HINTS

- Be sure to be watchful of very young children who put everything in their mouth during this activity.
- Be sure rocks are too large to be swallowed.

DEVELOPMENTAL GOALS

Develop creativity, small motor development, and hand-eye coordination; explore a new use for a familiar object; and explore a new form of sculpture design.

PREPARATION

Go outside and collect the rocks for this activity. Talk with the children about the rocks—their colors, shapes, sizes, lines and other details. Ask them to think about what they would like to make with the rocks. Wash and dry the rocks thoroughly.

PROCESS

1. Use one rock for a base.
2. Glue on a rock for a head or simply for another part of the sculpture.
3. Glue on other details with bits of trim and fabric.
4. Draw on details with markers or paint.

VARIATIONS

- Make a family of rock people.
- Make a zoo filled with rock animals.
- Make abstract sculptures out of rocks.
- Glue small pebbles onto paper boxes for unusual gifts.

NOTES FOR NEXT TIME: _____

_____

_____

_____

Salt Dough

MATERIALS

- ☐ 3/4 cup water
- ☐ 1 cup salt
- ☐ 1/2 cup cornstarch
- ☐ mixing spoon
- ☐ measuring cups
- ☐ aluminum foil
- ☐ pan
- ☐ stove or hot plate

💡 HELPFUL HINTS

- Constant adult supervision is necessary when cooking the dough. Keep children a safe watching distance from the stove top.

- Store leftover salt dough in a plastic bag. It will keep for a few days. Knead the dough before using it to make it pliable again.

DEVELOPMENTAL GOALS

Develop creativity, small motor development, and hand-eye coordination and explore a new use for crayons.

PREPARATION

Have the children help measure all ingredients. Let the the children taste the dry ingredients. Talk about how the ingredients taste.

PROCESS

1. Mix 1 cup salt, 3/4 cup water, and 1/2 cup cornstarch in a pan.
2. Cook over medium heat, stirring constantly until the mixture thickens into a doughy consistency.
3. Remove the mixture from the heat and cool on a piece of foil.
4. Have the child knead the dough thoroughly until it is soft and pliable.
5. Shape the dough into forms or objects.
6. The dough will dry hard without baking.

VARIATIONS

- Make decorations, pins, play fruit, beads, and letters from the salt dough.
- An adult or older children can brush on a coat of clear nail polish for a shiny finish.
- Add food coloring or liquid tempera for colored salt dough.

NOTES FOR NEXT TIME: _____

_____

_____

A

All Ages

Sawdust Sculptures

MATERIALS

- ☐ wallpaper paste
- ☐ water
- ☐ large mixing bowl
- ☐ mixing spoon
- ☐ sawdust

 **HELPFUL HINTS**

- The sawdust sculpture takes 2 or 3 days to dry.
- Store drying pieces in a safe place where they will not get knocked down during the drying period.
- Ask folks at a local lumberyard or home-decorating store to save sawdust for this activity.

DEVELOPMENTAL GOALS

Develop creativity, small motor development, and hand-eye coordination; explore a new kind of dough; and reinforce the recycling of sawdust for an art activity.

PREPARATION

Have at least 2 cups of sawdust for this recipe. Ask parents or friends to help accumulate it for this activity.

PROCESS

1. Mix the wallpaper paste and water to a thick, doughy consistency.
2. Add sawdust until the mixture can be formed into a ball.
3. Give each child a lump of the mixture to mold into any shape or form.
4. Dry the shapes for 2 or 3 days.

VARIATIONS

- Paint the dried shapes with tempera paint.
- Add toothpicks, buttons, and sequins for added details.

NOTES FOR NEXT TIME: _____

_____

_____

_____

Sculpture Bouquets

MATERIALS

☐ container to hold play dough (e.g., tin can, old vase, paper cup, margarine tub)

☐ play dough or clay

 **HELPFUL HINTS**

- Start by poking in the tallest pieces first; then use the short ones.

- Objects can be added later to the bouquet. It can be an ongoing display reflecting the seasons!

DEVELOPMENTAL GOALS

Develop creativity, small motor development, and hand-eye coordination; explore a new kind of three-dimensional sculpture material; and discuss such design concepts as size, shape, texture, and placement.

PREPARATION

Collect such natural objects as dried flowers, weeds, twigs, and leaves. Take the children on an outdoor walk for the fun of collecting objects for their sculpture bouquets.

PROCESS

1. Select a container in which to put the natural objects.

2. Put a lump of clay or play dough in the bottom of the container.

3. Squish down the clay or dough so it fills the bottom (or most of the bottom) of the container.

4. Begin the arrangement by poking one object into the dough.

5. Put in other pieces, one by one.

6. Try placing objects at various heights and angles.

7. Turn the sculpture around and look at it from all sides. Fill open spots.

VARIATIONS

- Use objects with different textures, colors, and shapes.

- Look for interesting objects, such as feathers and pine cones on pieces of branches, to add to the bouquet.

NOTES FOR NEXT TIME: _____

_____

_____

_____

3 Years Old and Up

Soap-Ball Sculptures

MATERIALS

- ☐ box of soap flakes
- ☐ bowl
- ☐ mixing spoon
- ☐ water
- ☐ wax paper

💡 HELPFUL HINT

- The sculpture can be taken apart and used as soap later.

DEVELOPMENTAL GOALS

Develop creativity, small motor development, and hand-eye coordination and explore a new kind of modeling material.

PREPARATION

Pour whole box of soap flakes into a large bowl.

PROCESS

1. Add water to the soap flakes until the mixture is the consistency of paste.
2. Working on a piece of wax paper, roll the mixture into balls.
3. Put the balls together for designs or objects.
4. Toothpicks help hold balls together.
5. Let the sculpture dry on a piece of wax paper.

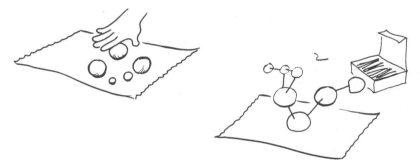

VARIATIONS

- Use pipe cleaners or toothpicks for arms.
- Use buttons, sequins, and beads for other details.
- Make soap balls to give as gifts.
- Make soap animals, flowers, and people.
- Add tempera paint for colorful soap balls.

NOTES FOR NEXT TIME: _____

_____

_____

Soapy Sculpture Dough

MATERIALS

- [ ] 2 cups soap flakes
- [ ] 2 tablespoons water
- [ ] large bowl
- [ ] mixing spoon
- [ ] measuring spoons and cups

 **HELPFUL HINTS**

- This dough is white and very pliable. Because it is very easy to manipulate, it is good for very young children just starting to use modeling materials.

- If a child accidentally gets a taste of the soap dough, help rinse the child's mouth with water until the taste is gone. If soap gets into the child's eye, flood the eye with clear water.

- This is a good material to carve with a spoon, a Popsicle stick, a toothpick or another tool.

- Be sure to talk about the physical changes children can see during the mixing and making of this dough.

DEVELOPMENTAL GOALS

Develop creativity, small motor development, and hand-eye coordination; explore a new kind of dough and reinforce the science concept of change in materials during mixing.

PREPARATION

Let children measure all ingredients.

PROCESS

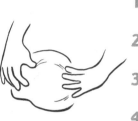

1. Add water slowly to the soap flakes until the mixture is the consistency of paste.
2. Let the children mix the materials to this consistency.
3. Form grapefruit-sized balls with lumps of the mixture.
4. Use the modeling soap to make any dough creation desired.

VARIATIONS

- Decorate soap-dough creations with toothpicks, pipe cleaners, buttons, and sequins.
- Add this soap-dough mixture to your modeling materials in the wintertime.
- Add food coloring for colored soap dough.
- Make the dough into soap balls or shapes to use at home or school, or give them as gifts.
- Make fragrant soap balls by adding vanilla or lemon extract or spices like cinnamon.

NOTES FOR NEXT TIME: _____

_____

_____

CLAY, PLAY DOUGH, AND MODELING MATERIALS

Copyright © 2004, Delmar Learning

Spicy Cinnamon Apple Dough

MATERIALS

- ☐ 1 cup ground cinnamon
- ☐ 1 cup applesauce
- ☐ 1/4 cup white glue
- ☐ bowl
- ☐ measuring cups
- ☐ spoon
- ☐ cutting board
- ☐ rolling pin
- ☐ cookie cutters
- ☐ Popsicle sticks
- ☐ plastic knives

💡 HELPFUL HINT

- Store the dough in a bowl covered with plastic wrap.

DEVELOPMENTAL GOALS

Develop creativity, small motor development, and hand-eye coordination; explore a new kind of play dough; and reinforce the science concepts of changes in materials through making the recipe.

PREPARATION

Remind the children that this dough is not edible! Have children measure out all ingredients. They can taste the materials before mixing them together.

PROCESS

1. Add cinnamon to applesauce until it is a clay-like consistency.
2. Add glue to thicken the mixture.
3. Mix until smooth and pliable.
4. Give each child a ball of dough to mold and shape.
5. Let the dough dry.

VARIATIONS

- Add glitter for a sparkly dough.
- Cut out letters, numbers, and shapes with Popsicle sticks or plastic knives.
- Cut out dough with cookie cutters.
- Decorate dough with buttons, sequins, and tiny rocks before setting out to dry.

NOTES FOR NEXT TIME: _____

_____

_____

_____

3
Years Old and Up

Spool Sculptures

MATERIALS

- [ ] spools (a variety of sizes)
- [ ] assorted fabric pieces
- [ ] markers
- [ ] glue
- [ ] sequins
- [ ] buttons
- [ ] feathers
- [ ] anything that will stimulate children's imaginations as decorations

💡 HELPFUL HINTS

- Ask a local tailor or dry cleaner to save spools for this activity.
- Remember that the younger the child, the larger the spools required.

DEVELOPMENTAL GOALS

Develop creativity, small motor development, and hand-eye coordination and explore a new use of spools as three-dimensional materials.

PREPARATION

Talk about the various spools. Discuss what they could become. ("What do their shapes remind you of?") Encourage all kinds of replies.

PROCESS

1. Use the spool as a body.
2. Glue on materials for clothes.
3. Alternatively, use the spool purely as a base of a decoration.
4. Draw details on the spool with markers.
5. Glue on bits and pieces of yarn and ribbon for other details.

VARIATIONS

- Make a spool family.
- Older children can create a group of characters from a favorite story or fairy tale.
- Make spool buildings, cars, or animals.

NOTES FOR NEXT TIME: _____

_____

_____

_____

4

Years Old and Up

String and Glue Sculptures

MATERIALS

☐ heavy string
☐ glue
☐ wax paper
☐ bowl

💡 HELPFUL HINTS

• The longer the piece of string, the more fun it will be to make a string sculpture. If you conduct this activity with children under age 4, however, use a string no longer than 12 inches.

• Because this activity involves waiting to see how the product turns out, it is most suitable for children aged 4 and up. Younger children will simply enjoy manipulating the string!

DEVELOPMENTAL GOALS

Develop creativity, small motor development, and hand-eye coordination and explore new kinds of sculpture materials.

PREPARATION

Dip the heavy string into a bowl of glue. Be sure the string is completely covered with glue.

PROCESS

1. Give each child a glue-soaked piece of string.
2. Form a shape with the string on wax paper.
3. Let the glue dry completely.
4. Remove the string sculpture from the wax paper.

VARIATIONS

• Add food color to the glue for a colorful string sculpture.
• Add glitter to the glue for a sparkly string sculpture.
• Hang on a string for a string sculpture mobile.
• Use different kinds of heavy string for different textures.
• Use small, medium, and long pieces of glue-soaked string.

NOTES FOR NEXT TIME: _____
_____
_____
_____

Stuffed Paper-Bag Sculptures

4 Years Old and Up

MATERIALS

- ☐ paper bags of various sizes
- ☐ newspaper
- ☐ tempera paint
- ☐ paintbrushes
- ☐ markers
- ☐ string or rubber bands
- ☐ wallpaper paste
- ☐ mixing bowl and spoon

HELPFUL HINTS

- Be sure to tell the children that this is a two-step process. Remind the children they will have to wait until the bags are completely dry before painting.

- Very young children enjoy simply stuffing the bag with paper and possibly doing a little bit of decorating, as well.

DEVELOPMENTAL GOALS

Develop creativity, small motor development, and hand-eye coordination and explore a new three-dimensional media.

PREPARATION

Wad newspapers into balls. Tear other pieces of newspaper into strips. Mix wallpaper paste according to directions on package.

PROCESS

1. Fill a paper bag with wads of newspaper.
2. Close the bag with piece of string or rubber band.
3. Dip strips of newspaper into the wallpaper paste.
4. Pull the newspaper strip between two fingers to remove excess paste.
5. Wrap the strip around the paper bag
6. Continue adding strips, forming such details as arms, a nose, ears, and a tail.
7. Let the bag dry completely before painting or decorating it with markers or crayons.

VARIATIONS

- Cover milk cartons, tissue boxes, oatmeal boxes, and other containers with paper strips. Dry and then paint.
- Glue on yarn for hair, buttons for eyes, and fabric and trim scraps for clothing details.

NOTES FOR NEXT TIME: _____

_____

CLAY, PLAY DOUGH, AND MODELING MATERIALS

Styrofoam Sculptures

MATERIALS

- ☐ Styrofoam of various sizes and shapes, such as sheets, broken parts of packaging materials, "peanuts," etc.
- ☐ white glue
- ☐ pieces of cardboard (optional)
- ☐ toothpicks
- ☐ scraps of fabric, trim
- ☐ ribbon
- ☐ markers
- ☐ tempera paint
- ☐ brushes

HELPFUL HINT

- Some children may insist on making "something" out of the Styrofoam rather than an abstract design. This is perfectly o.k. Try to encourage them to make a "creative something!"

DEVELOPMENTAL GOALS

Develop creativity, small motor development, and hand-eye coordination and explore a new three-dimensional material.

PREPARATION

Talk with the children about the collection of Styrofoam. Discuss size and shape of the pieces. Ask the children to think about what they would like to create with these pieces.

PROCESS

1. Use a piece of cardboard or sheet of Styrofoam as a base.
2. Glue pieces of Styrofoam onto the base.
3. Use toothpicks to add small pieces to the design.
4. Continue gluing on pieces until satisfied with the design.

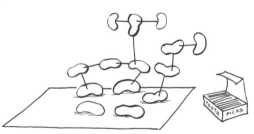

VARIATIONS

- Use markers to draw details on the sculpture.
- Paint the sculpture with tempera paint.
- Glue on pieces of fabric, trim, and ribbon for interesting effects.

NOTES FOR NEXT TIME: _____

_____

_____

_____

A
All Ages

Uncooked Play Dough

MATERIALS

- ☐ 3 cups flour
- ☐ 1 cup water
- ☐ 1/4 cup salt
- ☐ 1 tablespoon oil
- ☐ coloring
- ☐ spoon for mixing
- ☐ measuring cups and spoons

💡 HELPFUL HINTS

- The deeper the dishpan, the less mess.
- Store dough in the refrigerator in a closed container.
- Take the play dough out early in the day so it is at room temperature when used. It is more pliable and fun to work with at room temperature.

DEVELOPMENTAL GOALS

Develop creativity, small motor development, and hand-eye coordination and explore science concepts while making play dough.

PREPARATION

Gather all materials. Have a deep plastic dishpan available for mixing ingredients. Let the children help with the measuring and mixing. Talk about the changes in materials as they are mixed. Talk about how the flour looks dry, then how it looks mixed with the water and with the oil. Use words like *dry* and *liquid*, as well as the correct words for the measurements of materials.

PROCESS

1. Mix the flour and salt.
2. Add water with coloring and oil gradually.
3. Add more water if too stiff.
4. Add more flour if too sticky.
5. Store the dough in plastic bags or a covered container.

VARIATIONS

- Prepare two recipes in two dishpans. Make each a different color.
- Shake in cinnamon, ground cloves, or peppermint extract for interesting smells.
- Divide the recipe into several smaller bowls to make several colors of dough.

NOTES FOR NEXT TIME: _____

_____

Yummy Play Dough

MATERIALS

- ☐ creamy peanut butter
- ☐ marshmallow crème
- ☐ graham cracker crumbs
- ☐ wax paper
- ☐ bowls
- ☐ spoons
- ☐ plastic knives

 **HELPFUL HINTS**

- Check for peanut allergies before conducting this activity.
- Be sure children wash hands before mixing the recipe and before shaping the dough.
- Because this is such a simple recipe, it is great for very young artists!
- Remember to talk about each of the ingredients—its smell, texture, color, and taste before, during, and after mixing.

DEVELOPMENTAL GOALS

Develop creativity, small motor development, and hand-eye coordination; explore a new kind of play dough; and reinforce the science concepts of changing materials through mixing the dough.

PREPARATION

Instruct the children to wash their hands. Let the children feel the smoothness of both the peanut butter and the marshmallow crème.

PROCESS

1. Mix equal parts of peanut butter and marshmallow crème in a bowl.
2. Stir until smooth and pliable. Children can help do this.
3. With clean hands, mold into shapes or designs on wax paper surface.
4. Roll in graham-cracker crumbs.
5. Let set for an hour or so.
6. Enjoy!

VARIATIONS

- Use chunky peanut butter. Talk about the difference it makes in the dough.
- Use tools to cut out the dough into shapes, letters, and numbers.

NOTES FOR NEXT TIME: _____

_____

_____

_____

Edible Doughs

PEANUT BUTTER NO-COOK DOUGH

1 cup peanut butter

1 cup Karo syrup

1-1/4 cups nonfat dry milk solids

1 cup sifted confectioners sugar

1. Blend peanut butter and syrup in large mixing bowl.
2. Mix dry milk and sifted confectioners sugar together.
3. Mix all together—first with a spoon and then with the hands.
4. Turn onto board and continue kneading until mixture is well blended and smooth.
5. Give each child a ball of dough to knead and shape.
6. To make cut-out cookies, roll dough to 1/2 inch thickness.

HONEY DOUGH

3 tablespoons honey

4 tablespoons peanut butter

1/2 cup nonfat dry milk

1/4 cup dry cereal flakes (crushed)

1. Mix honey and peanut butter in bowl.
2. Gradually add nonfat dry milk. Mix well.
3. Give each child a pat of butter or margarine to grease their hands.
4. Give child a lump of dough to shape into balls or any other desired form.
5. Roll balls or shapes in dry cereal flakes.
6. Chill until firm.

EASY FUDGE DOUGH

1/4 cup butter

1/4 cup sweetened condensed milk

1 teaspoon vanilla,

1 pound confectioners' sugar

3/4 cup cocoa

1/4 teaspoon salt

1. Melt butter in a saucepan (or in the microwave for 10 seconds on HIGH).
2. Stir in milk and vanilla.
3. Gradually add mixture of sugar, cocoa, and salt.
4. Mix until soft and creamy.
5. Give each child a spoonful of fudge to mold with hands.
6. Put molded fudge on piece of wax paper and chill.
7. Eat and enjoy!

MARY'S DOUGH

1 egg

1-1/2 cups cups warm water

1 package yeast

1 teaspoon salt

1 tablespoon sugar

4 cups flour

1. Pour 1-1/2 cups warm water into the bowl.
2. Sprinkle the yeast into the water and stir until it is dissolved.
3. Add salt, sugar, and flour. Mix together to form a ball.
4. Sprinkle flour onto the work surface and place dough on it.
5. Let the children knead the dough until it is smooth and elastic.
6. Encourage the children to roll and twist the dough into shapes.
7. Place the dough sculptures on the cookie sheet and cover it with a clean towel. Place in warm area to rise.
8. After dough designs have doubled in size, brush each one with beaten egg.
9. Cook dough in 350-degree oven for 12 to 15 minutes until they are firm and golden brown.
10. Remove from oven, cool, and enjoy!

POTATO DOUGH

1/3 cup mashed potatoes

1-3/4 cups powdered sugar

1 teaspoon vanilla

2 cups flaked coconut

1. Mix ingredients in a bowl thoroughly.
2. Give each child a lump of potato dough on a piece of wax paper.
3. Shape into desired shape.
4. Place in refrigerator until very cool.

YUMMY PLAY DOUGH

creamy peanut butter

marshmallow crème

graham cracker crumbs

1. Mix equal parts of peanut butter and marshmallow crème together in bowl.
2. Stir until smooth and pliable. Children can help do this.
3. With clean hands, mold into shapes or designs on wax paper surface.
4. Roll in graham cracker crumbs.
5. Let set for an hour or so.
6. Enjoy!

Index by Ages